What if...

by The Students of 5/6 Springvale Elementary

To Troy Yeo, Terrilee Bulger,
Ms Dockendorff, Sandra
Falkenham and
The Earth

All authors proceeds from this book will be donated to charities that make a difference in our community and abroad. Take a look at:

Kiva.org
Ryanswell.ca
Org.kidshelpphone.ca/en/atlantic/halifax
Metro.spca.ca
WWF.ca

Some of the student's paintings were inspired by Canadian artist Ted Harrison.

The publisher acknowledges the support of the Government of Canada through the Canada Book Fund of the Department of Canadian Heritage and the Canada Council for the Arts Block Grant Program.

Printed and Bound in Canada
978-1-894838-65-8

What if...

y Students of 5/6 Springvale Elementary

...the world looked like this?

What if children
had a place
to talk about
their problems
face to face?

What if everyone
felt like they had
a friend?

What if teased kids all felt safe from anybody any place? What if people weren't so cruel to any person in any school?

What if we protected our clear blue lakes, fresh misty harbours, and clean oceans shimmering under the bright sparkling moon?

What if kids weren't judged by how much money their parents had?

What if all pets were safe from harm?
What if all animals could have a home?

What if the seas were
clean and playing
dolphins could be seen?

What if all oceans were pollution free? That would make the fish as happy as can be.

What if the
internet were
only used
for good?

What if
there was no
such thing
as war and
the world
was peaceful
evermore?

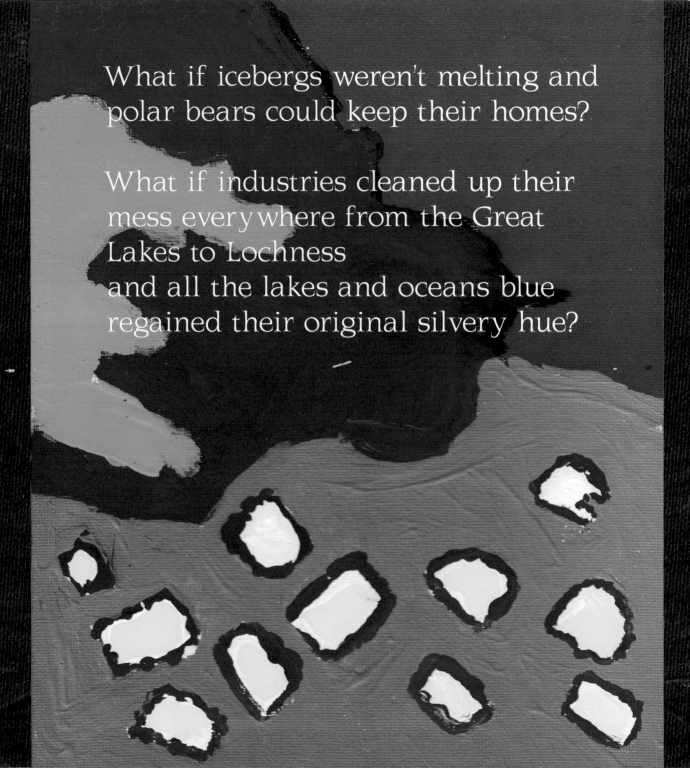

What if icebergs weren't melting and
polar bears could keep their homes?

What if industries cleaned up their
mess everywhere from the Great
Lakes to Lochness
and all the lakes and oceans blue
regained their original silvery hue?

What if people put
their garbage in the
trash
and not in the rivers
or on the grass?

What if wildlife had a
home
where their young were
safe to roam?

What if no one ever
bullied anyone or anything
and peace were to bloom like
a blossom in the spring?

What if we kept the earth clean
and put litter where it is supposed
to be?

What if recycling were an act
and we all made a pact?

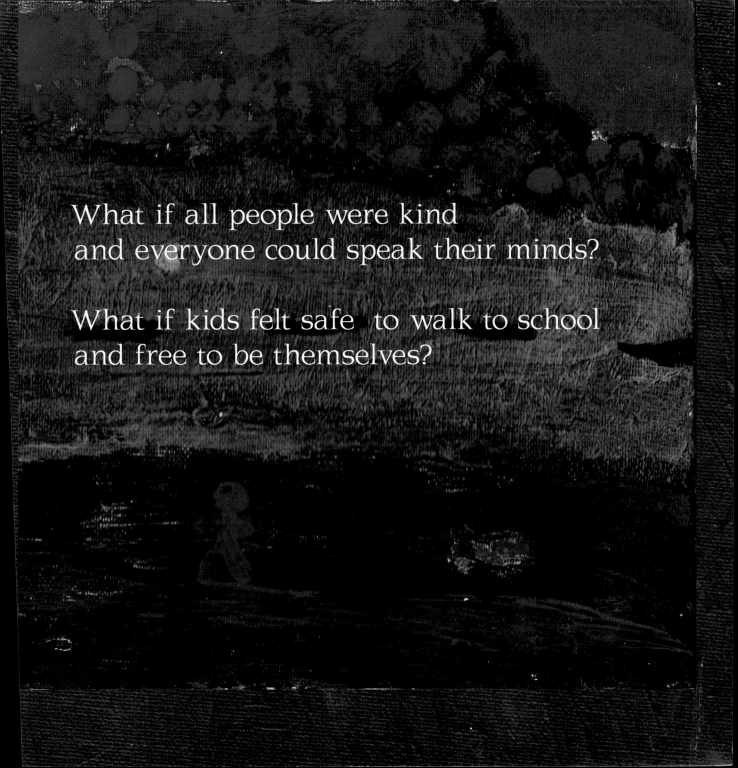

What if all people were kind
and everyone could speak their minds?

What if kids felt safe to walk to school
and free to be themselves?

What if the oceans were perfectly
clean polluted not by man or
machine?

What if no one felt the need
to cut down all the trees?

What if clean water was not a chore
and plenty was found through
every door? And everyone had
enough to drink
with some left over for bathroom
and kitchen sink?

What if more people made a loan to help others build a home?

What if everyone gave a hand to buy a goat or a hen?

What if boys and girls had
equal rights and all kids
were free to learn and play?
And families had fresh water
every day
so kids could go to school?

What if we had a peaceful world,
a world of peace?

Please visit our blog if you would like more information on how you can make a differ-ence. Check out the various tips and websites offering information on our blog. Also make a pledge to treat others and the earth with kindness! pledgeforkindness.blogspot.com

Authors and Illustrators: Drew, Emaysia, Matteo, Nicol Owen, AJ, Colin, Christian, Basmala, Faye, Dora, Tim, Jessica, Kelly, Ethan, Erich, Serena, and Jade